A Special Gift

presented to:

....

from:

....

date:

....

a little book of

hugs™

for
Mom

Inspiration for the Heart

**Andrews McMeel
Publishing**

Kansas City

ISBN: 0-7407-1183-0

Library of Congress Catalog Card Number: 00-102159

Messages by G.A. Myers
Personalized Scriptures by LeAnn Weiss
Interior design by LinDee Loveland and Vanessa Bearden
Project Editor: Philis Boultinghouse

CONTENTS

I remember, I remember
The house where
I was born
The little window
where the sun
Came peeping in at morn.

—THOMAS HOOD

CHAPTER ONE

a Mother's Love

Cultivate faith, goodness,
knowledge, self-control,
perseverance, godliness,

brotherly kindness, and love
in your children. For if they
are growing in these qualities,
they won't be ineffective or
unproductive, and they will
never stumble.

Love,

Your Living God

2 Peter 1:5-11

*Y*ou may not realize it, but
you are a gifted gardener.
Though you may be
incapable of keeping a
simple houseplant alive,
you are an accomplished
gardener nonetheless.

*B*ut the soil you work in is not of this world. No! It is the soil of the human heart.

*Y*our children are your
fertile field, and in their
hearts you have planted
your seeds of love, joy,
peace, patience, kindness,
goodness, faithfulness,
gentleness, and
self-control.

*Y*ou have courageously
protected your precious
field from destructive and
uninvited strangers.
When spiritual or physical
disease threatened, you
worked with bleeding
hands to free the roots of
life from contaminants.

*Y*ou have nursed the
wounds left by the
violent storms of life.
You have struggled
through seasons of
drought; you have
celebrated at the sight
of unhampered growth.

*Y*ou have weeded,
watered, plowed,
and prayed.

*I*n turn, you should know
that your labor of love has
not gone unnoticed. You
are deeply loved and
appreciated—not only
by hearts you have tended,
but by the God who made
you the mother (and
expert gardener) you are.

$\mathcal{G}$od bless you, Mom.

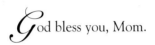

There never was a woman like her. She was gentle as a dove and brave as a lioness.... The memory of my mother and her teachings were, after all, the only capital I had to start life with, and on that capital I have made my way.

—ANDREW JACKSON

CHAPTER TWO

a Mother's Classroom

Your teachings have great importance! What you teach guides your children when they walk and watches over them while they sleep. Your instructions are lights for their lives and speak to them even when you aren't there.

Love,

Your God of Wisdom

Proverbs 6:20–23

You may not have a
professional degree, but
you are a world-class
teacher all the same. And
you practice your profession
on a daily basis—not on a
college campus or behind a
podium in a marble-floored
classroom—but right there
in the warmth of your
carefully kept home.

*W*hile you've gone
about the rigorous routines
of motherhood, little eyes
have watched, and little
minds and hearts have
been shaped for eternity.

*Y*our young pupils have
learned of sacrificial love
as they've seen you take
the last and least so others
can have more. They've
learned to distinguish
right from wrong as
they've observed your life
of honesty and integrity.

They've learned about faith as they've heard you pray to an unseen God—sometimes in tears, sometimes with thanksgiving, always with a firm belief that God is real, that He hears your prayers, and that He responds faithfully.

They've learned that failure is not final as they've seen you confess your own faults and offer generous forgiveness to others.

*A*bove all, they've learned
what real love means—it
means sharing hurts, hopes,
joys, and homecomings; it
means staying when it would
be easier to leave, defending
when others accuse, holding
on when you're tempted to let
go, and letting go when you
desperately want to hold on.

*T*he same lips that
have countless times
formed the word
Mom will say,

"Thanks, Mom, for
your precious teachings.
You're the best."

My mother was the most
beautiful woman I ever saw.
All I am I owe
to my mother.
I attribute all my success
in life to the moral,
intellectual, and physical
education I received from her.

—GEORGE WASHINGTON

If you can't make it better,
you can laugh at it.

—ERMA BOMBECK

a Mother's Faith

Fan the flame of My gift in your children. Sincere faith can be passed on to your

children and to their children
from generation to
generation. Keep passing on a
heritage of faith. Don't let
My flame go out!

Love,
Your 100%
Faithful God

2 Timothy 1:5–6

When it comes to matters of eternity, moms have a special sense. Somehow moms can see beyond disheveled hair, freshly torn jeans, and smudged faces.

Moms can look into
the tearful eyes of an
unhappy two-year-old
or the questioning eyes
of a moody teenager
and see not only what
is—but what can be.

As you interact with
your children in your
daily routines—routines
that may seem mundane
and far removed from
eternity—remember that
you are imparting a
sense of something
much bigger than the
here and now.

*Y*ou are imparting seeds of faith. As your children watch you react to sadness, joy, tragedy, success, and failure, they begin to learn what it means to have faith in something beyond themselves.

*Y*our gentle reassurance when things go wrong, your unfailing confidence in the face of apparent failure, your ability to trust God when life seems to be falling apart—these responses give faith structure and meaning. You are the "embodiment" of faith—faith "with skin on."

*E*very new day presents
opportunities to pass on
little bits of your faith—
little bits of eternity.
Enjoy a beautiful sunset
together and remind your
children of the God who
made it.

When hearts get broken or dreams fall apart, remind them that God holds the key to real happiness and that He is the rebuilder of hopes and dreams. When uncertainty clouds their vision, lead them to their knees in prayer—pray with them often and about everything.

When Satan wins a battle, wrap your arms around them, gently embrace confidence back into them, and tell them of God's unconditional love—a love that will love them no matter what. When it comes to matters of eternity… moms have a special sense.

I believe the most valuable contribution a parent can make to his child is to instill in him a genuine faith in God.

—DR. JAMES DOBSON

a Mother's Encouragement

*Encourage and build up
your family daily. Help them
identify and get rid of everything that hinders them and the
sin that so easily entangles*

*them. Challenge them to run
with endurance the race of life
I've already marked out for
them. Give them courage!*

Love,

Your God Who
Gives You Endurance
and Encouragement

1 Thessalonians 5:11;
Hebrews 3:13; 12:1; Romans 15:5

A word of encouragement from Mom takes the *im* out of *impossible*, the *'t* out of *can't*, and the *un* out of *unable*.

A cheerful word
from Mom can turn
impending failure
into success and can
spur a child on to
finish a seemingly
impossible task.

*T*his world can be a
frightening place—
classroom assignments,
playground bullies, music
recitals, competitive
sports—such challenges
often require the courage
of David facing Goliath.

*A*t times like these,
children—both young
and old—need the gift
of courage. And that's
what *encouragers* do—
they impart *courage*—
and moms are some of
the best encouragers
in the world.

*J*ust a few simple
words from you give
your children courage
to meet the challenges
at hand:

"*I* believe in you."
"You can do it."
"You are so special."
"I am so proud of you."
"Keep going…
keep fighting…
keep believing."

This world is full of people
and events that drain faith
and spirit from your family,
but God has given you the
ability to fight off these
enemies with loving words
of encouragement. Never
underestimate their power.

*W*atch your children's backs straighten, their eyes brighten, their work improve, their lives change, and their love deepen—all because you have imparted courage to them by your words.

Every time we encourage someone, we give them a transfusion of courage.

—CHARLES SWINDOLL

CHAPTER 5 FIVE

a Mother's Hope

You are worth far more than rubies! You lack nothing of value. You bring good to every day. You work vigorously, and your life is profitable. You are clothed with strength and dignity! You can laugh at life. You speak with wisdom and faithful instruction; you juggle numerous roles and use your time wisely.

Your children arise and call you blessed, and your husband also praises you! Many women do noble things, but you surpass them all! Others also see what you do and admire your work as a mom.

Love,

Your God Who Praises You for Fearing Me

Proverbs 31:10–30

*T*have an important
message for you. It
may come as a surprise,
because this message
is not repeated nearly
often enough. Are
you ready?

You are greatly
admired. It's
worth repeating.
You are greatly
admired.

*A*nd not just by your family—by others too. Some of your admirers are close acquaintances; others are strangers. But they all hold you in high regard. Why? Because you are a mother through and through, in and out, and all about.

*B*ecause you are
totally in love with
your family and are
thoroughly prepared
to show your love by
giving all, asking little,
and accepting less.

*B*ecause you have become an expert at being in three places at one time, because you are a tender nurse with a sick child, because you are a diplomatic disciplinarian, because you are a mighty warrior against the forces of evil that threaten your home.

*B*ecause you see the amazing potential in the hearts and minds of awkward, and sometimes annoying, boys and girls.

*P*lease disregard any
previous messages you may
have received that gave
the impression that you
were not highly valued
and greatly respected. You
are a rich and treasured
gift from God.

You may do many other things in your life on earth that will be productive and meaningful, but none will be as admired as being the beautiful mother you are.

Who ran to help me
when I fell
And would some pretty
story tell,
Or kiss the place to make it
well? My mother.

—ANN TAYLOR

Look for these other little *Hugs* books:

A Little Book of Hugs for Friends
A Little Book of Hugs for Sisters
A Little Book of Hugs for Women
A Little Book of Hugs for Teachers
A Little Book of Hugs to Encourage and Inspire

Also look for these full-size *Hugs* books:

Hugs for Women
Hugs for Friends
Hugs for Mom
Hugs for Kids
Hugs for Teachers
Hugs for Sisters
Hugs for Those in Love
Hugs for the Hurting
Hugs for Grandparents
Hugs for Dad
Hugs for the Holidays
Hugs to Encourage and Inspire